THE SPIDER'S TOUCH

The Spider's Touch is the first full-length collection of poems by a poet with a surprising range of voices, themes and forms. Michael Cayley was born in 1950 and has lived most of his life in Hove, Sussex. He read English at St. John's College, Oxford, where he developed a strong interest in Verlaine and the late Symbolists. He is now working as a Civil Servant in London.

Michael Cayley's first booklet collection of poems, *Moorings*, was published by Carcanet Press in 1971. He edited a selection of the poems of Richard Crashaw for Carcanet's Fyfield Books Series.

The Spider's Touch

by Michael Cayley

'The spider taketh hold with her hands,
and is in kings' palaces.'—*Proverbs*

A CARCANET PRESS PUBLICATION

To George Cornelius

Acknowledgements are due to *Carcanet*, 'Poetry Now' (BBC Radio Three), *Southern Arts Review*, and *Tribune*, where some of these poems first appeared.

A few of the poems included here were first published in *Moorings* (Carcanet Press 1971). My thanks are due to Dr. John Carey and to Michael Schmidt for their advice, and to Jay for checking the final manuscript.

First published 1973
by Carcanet Press Ltd.
266 Councillor Lane
Cheadle Hulme
Cheadle, Cheshire

Printed in Great Britain
by W & J Mackay Limited, Chatham

CONTENTS

I. *Timothy*
The Way Home   9
After the Party   10
In the Shopping-centre   11
Uncle Timothy's Excursion   12
On the Quay   13
Leave-taking   14
Timothy's Grandmother   15
Dawn Chorus   16
Timothy's Evening   17
Timothy and Eve   18
Eve and Timothy   19
Timothy Recollects   20
Timothy's Son   21
Eve's Brother   22
Timothy in a Café   23
The Voice   24
Timothy's Bedside   26

II.
Monument   29
December   30
Slave-trader   31
Naval Officers   32
The Seaside   33
Mammoth   34
Tyrolean Festival   35
Toad   36
Thumb-nail   37

III. *Chénier in Prison*   39

IV. *Catch a Falling Star*
Robbie's Funeral   49
Runway   50
Aerobatics   51
The Reporters   52
Maps   53
Seductress   54
Testing, Testing   55

The Tightrope   56
Casualties   57
Symphony   58
The Pool   59
A London Square   60
Promenade   61
If Only   62
Huntress   63
The Car   64

I. TIMOTHY

The sun is set, the spring is gone.
Thomas Gray

i. The Way Home

Walking the bike
up the hill. Sorting stars
into constellations. The moon
segmented by bare twigs
into rough triangles and rhombuses.
Trees lopped to trunks
by slabs of concrete.
A mastiff parades
furrows of future walls.

ii. *After The Party*

Half-drunk, no doubt, but still his gloved hands
keep the car straight or swing with the road
round fields. A brief three hours
had advanced gear from dance to kiss to pet
but now, having kissed her goodnight
by roses trained up her bungalow's porch,
he does not know her name, just the memory
of skin and nervous hands.
                              The cars drawn up
on the verge or by field-gates at times
almost caress each other with bumpers:
no need to stare for their lovers' oblivion.
He follows the cat's-eyes towards the city lights,
accelerates into a lame bird, slows,
senses it mashed with blood, and smiles on.

He stares in pyjamas at squared wallpaper
lit by the streetlamp through thin curtains.
His drawing-roomed dog's barks strain
towards passing leashed bitches.

iii. In The Shopping-centre

Secure in the anonymity
of shapely legs, they rush on
their shopping, apparently unaware
of leers lounged against bus-stops
and display windows. Their elegance
yields no suggestion of segregated

giggling with sisters and confidantes
over the whistling of a
councillor at his climacteric or
the elevation of a
vicar's brows. Brought up with it all,
I note the rôles, smirk at recollections

of my own tentative incursions
into post-lapsarian
fairylands: the shopgirl sweeping back blonde
hair from her eyes as I glanced
from the highbrow indigestibles
to memorise for bedtime meditation

brash tits; the faces severely fixed
on riots, advice on slimming;
flushed goosestepping home through a world of thighs. . . .
Yes, girls still avert faces
from my balding celibacy, but
the younger already confront my over-

estimated age. Getting sweet on
the merely glimpsed in a bus
stopped years ago, and nightly computation
of pudenda has yielded
to the more responsible figures
which do not distract from tendering the right fares.

iv. Uncle Timothy's Excursion

Escorted by manikin spies, he has brushed off
the winter's hearthside ease. Their eyes creep round him
to pounce on a walled garden or a bag
swollen with purchases in a stranger's clench.
He hugs their ardent shoulders, softly satisfies
shrill interrogations. Insulated
and cuddly like a polar bear he looks
with greyed eyes from his nephews to a daffodil sun.

Crouched firm on concrete, he tends rigging, shoots
a schooner across the pond. It lurches, veers
wildly in a gust. Sunny voices tell
how his wife and daughters have plopped overboard
half-way to America. Brisk with hope, he directs
an air-and-sea search. The ship tacks to berth,
is cradled into dry dock. Clergymen now,
they offer solace as he muses home, bereft,
to the armchair undulations of the stock market report.

v. On The Quay

The sunset is held in the dock
beneath cranes shaking
languorous giraffe heads.

Gold ripples in the warm breeze seem to presage
my own progress to moneyed death.

I perambulate with a half-bald nephew
waving his angelic rattle
at passers-by.
            Beside their brother
the boys moored to my cuffs look smug
in their feet's worldly wisdom.

The quay too well-known to hunt warehouse secrets
or try their balance on straining cables,
they pry about my celibacy,
but I point to wavering masts,
talk of my dinghy days, and push on
through the summer, through bikini-clad
admirers of my baby namesake.

vi. Leave-taking

So common a sight retards no suitcases
or punching of tickets, demands
no momentary quizzing from porters' eyes.

As you roll away, you seem to say 'Cheese'
for a camera, gargoyle head
jutting from the carriage.
                                  I mouth 'Cheese' back,
unembarrassed for once by my well-stopped teeth,
and turn down the platform whose emptiness
the wind frosts.
                          But 'Cheese' I shape
for the ticket collector as the barrier
guillotines my shadow. Arms akimbo,
he contemplates. Then 'Cheese'. 'Cheese.'

Passengers pound off the snow and swing like pendulums
from foot to foot, but swing to a stop
as I stroll past. Stiff upper lips
melt into 'Cheese'. Our last kiss
was nothing to this promiscuous union
of the mouths of the whole station. Even the trains
relax.
            I scarf myself
and move to the bus-stop, mouthing 'Cheese. Say "Cheese".'

vii. Timothy's Grandmother

Legs brittle as twigs
bear the scars of the Blitz,
the sallow weariness
past caring how the wind
raids smutty hair.
Bygone romances
written into her palm
curl blindly
over the white stick
round which her dress
swirls in drab volumes
of past fashion. Undressing,
she dares the moth to do its worst
to knickers, eases herself
onto a stool. Toothlessly
she muses over coins whose hoarding
guarded memory from the new.

viii. Dawn Chorus

The curtains were willed to us
by my grandmother. Their faded velvet
hangs in folds round the dawn
they sieve. I switch off the hysterical
monotone of the alarm, roll over
to find no repose in your eyes
which blink chores into unfeeling being.

We jerk into the uniforms of day,
unveil the prospect so admired when we first
inherited it. Birds trilling dewy feathers
in the grandeur of historic trees perforate
our ears and die
into the chink of the family silver,
the clasping of a briefcase, my parting peck.

ix. Timothy's Evening

Fragments of lives flash past
on doorsteps or pavements, impersonal
as streetlamps. I sound my horn,
shift gear with the easy calculation of years.

I slam the door on unobserved figures,
embrace my wife and the semi-detached
figures earned. Stairs fall behind.
Trees' winter geometry is phased out with curtains
as I hum from a Bach chorale and see
my hands aspire at the altar rail.

Sleek on the sofa, I feel my neck and paunch—
the flesh fasting and twice-weekly communion
cannot keep down. My power failing,
and anyway blasé about desire,
I sing hymns in bed, leave my wife restless,
and seek an ivory tower where nightingales
pipe visions into my eager sleep.

x. Timothy And Eve

But his nails and teeth
could not bite her into life.

The years of squatting by toy bricks,
stooping over jig-saws
for his sister's children,
had dismantled the delicacy of lips,
coarsened and swelled fingers his religion
had secured from seductions.

Alone, at least there'd been no fear
of a partner like a tombstone
against his awkward gentleness, no need
to dive into booze, scratch and press
her body into union or lurch
the streets for prostitutes.
                              On Sundays
he blasphemed at this reward for past strictness,
watched his wife and children sprawl
over plastic building-sites,
and nursed his head
to hammocked anticipation
of empty rooms
and silence
restored to scuffed lawns.

xi. Eve And Timothy

That summer the scars alone
had been opaque to the tanning sun.

Laughing to herself,
she frightens the children with a werewolf

and mops their tears at promises
to be good. The leaves

flurry and sink in the yard.
Darning into the small hours, afraid.

xii. Timothy Recollects

Behind us the French water-garden
nibbled at its stone
confines beneath the marble stare
of heroes, and the organ
inscribed ancestors
on stagnant air.

We kicked aside with blind feet
magnolia blossom
crisped on the sunned path,
moved onto dry turf and drank in
the artificial lake defying
the May drought.

Even now we did not query
the guides' ready smiles
or the well-spoken servants
who had brought us tea
and paraded souvenir dusters.

We locked lids
against your teenage scrag
and gate-pillars chalked
with crude hearts: we sucked and stroked
dreams into life.

xiii. Timothy's Son

Goodness knows how she ended up.
At seven it was easy
to accept: I retreated with my brother
into snakes and ladders. When mum left
we sniffed the quiet.
It grew familiar as the playroom curtains.

In my early teens dad sometimes kissed us
to premature bed. An hour or two
and our ears would strain for a girl giggling
into the lounge. Next day I might find
perfume hanging round the sofa, rearrange
chairs and cushions, and have to humour
seething breakfast.
I smirked with schoolfriends and did not bedevil
my sex-play with questions.

Now dad's chucked work in, it tells, his having
no woman to run him. He asks more
than others' old men: insists
on a chamber-pot though he walks well enough;
won't tidy his litter. Rich, and, true,
he'd keep us comfortable even without my working.

At the time I didn't realise she shouted
in more than play when I prodded
bruises with infant fingers.
I don't know, though, going off
could have soothed her right.
                              My first memory of dad
he burnt a finger on his left hand
to the bone, still watched
the firework's second or so of flame.
Guy Fawkes calls no brief stars from me.
I keep to safety matches
as slow arms prop, inch me down to light the gas fire.

xiv. Eve's Brother

No, Eve never moped over
her husband's name, let alone lamented
into letters to him. The swords she drew
on the pink wallpaper might
suggest to a psychologist's cool
probing a little. . . —

Though, with their even spacing,
it was surely well under her thumb, the
ache for passion, or channelled into stock
escapism, reading cheap love-
stories. A marriage sinking to oaths,
blows, must have restrained

desire for a flesh-and-blood
substitute for her former prop and stay.
There were, we knew, casual nights in budding
directors' suave penthouses
till her face coarsened with crow's-feet and
her cycle slowed to

barrenness. Bridge champion then,
she gulped cup on tea-cup, her wish statute
when we chose partners, even for informal
rubbers. . . . Those of us now left
have to guard appearances! I must
get my white hair trimmed.

xv. Timothy In A Café

I simper thanks at the waitress' woollen bust
and the exhibitions of aware sirens,

hastily retreat into an exemplary age,
deflect my eyes with the expected shyness.

The café exhales ceaselessly. I too curl smoke
at the pane, knock ash onto mats puddly with coffee.

I note outside girls squelching
in booted legs, snowballs' trajectories,

scarved boys skidding with the unstable
shrieks of midget sisters. In the snow

they are careless of the ways we paved,
the smutted walls we bricked round them.

Retired into coronaries and rheumatism,
we watch what they make of our bequest.

Only with their teens do their faces crease
beside sweethearts' hair with responsibilities

and mind their icy step. Like the flakes
which worm down the window, they are unsure

how they will reach the propped shuffling
of grey nonentity I represent.

I down my coffee with scalding bravado
to slam the door on this mutual observation,

trudge away, and bury my head in my shoulders
against the cold, wading unsteadily.

Cars halt. Young mothers' arms hasten me over,
mindless of their film-star beauty. This watchful contempt

will not end until trim unfamiliar relatives
drive from the shovelling sexton to maisonnettes.

xvi. The Voice

I could note the voice below
on staves. Just the music
of its questioning
survives the floorboards.

The walls, papered with pastel
rectangles, don't assert
their bounding. The hands
tick round the alarm's

luminous green integers
unnoticed. The cream door
always invites—though
I cannot open.

Bed has, of course, its good points:
waking to breakfast trays. . . .
But you soon get tired
of pulling a cord

every time you want to pee.
To take up knitting, sort
flowers into vases,
is something when each

step tantalises, echoes
with walkers I merely
imagine. Even
of sounds I cannot

be certain, unconfirmed by
sight: do children really
tiff there, and scream at
my daughter's curbing?

And this voice, unvaried, which
has ousted the T.V.?
Every night my ears
strain over the bed,

suck in vain for the words, and
sink back, pillowed, from those
eager rhythms. What right
have I to get wheeled

to the lift, to barge in, vaunt
my uselessness?
                    Better
to keep quiet than risk
a madhouse. . . . Suburbs

don't make for thrillers' tortures.
Better to stick to safe
ground, to keep snoring
through such counterpoint.

xvii. Timothy's Bedside

He bears it well, joking himself
away from the pain of arthritis,
the body two heart-attacks have drained of self-support.
You have to lever his legs up and round,
to become a live walking-stick,
and his fingers clack knitting-needles slower
than the last visit, yet he stops impatience
in the throat's bottle-neck. Watching him pick up
stitches which vague eyes
had passed over, one can but hope
one's own nineties will escape bedwetting
for mere snatching at names buried
just out of worn sight. Not stubborn
against the nurse's buttressing arm,
he concentrates on balancing a tea-cup,
quickly covers up slipped allusions
to the voice he seems to hear question
non-stop, and lies back, eyes closed,
unaware of his grandchildren's mimicking.

II.

His skin yellows—book of life
and death—on its decaying monument.
Stones crumble, and their dust chokes
the passages. Broom and flue-brush
raise a blizzard of grit. Unrefreshed,
thought stales, bone brittles.
One by one the pages fall, to fragment at a breath.

December

Always she embroiders at the window,
safe in her grass-green armchair
from compact clouds like oakum and soot
and this wind which clutches the plain
tonelessly. Leaves which grazed walls
no longer couch like open hands,

but have been damped into earth. The other
nearby windows watch across
ledges. Two nuns come from the doctor's,
the verger's gone to the vicar,
the roadmen have pumped the drains
clear of scum, the solicitor

strides with his noon greetings and does not look
where the spider's star is spun
on her upper glass. When the vicar
brings sweet nothings to sunday tea
until the street is lit up,
they never refer to the clothes

she brushes and folds daily, though she calls
the man that left her stony
as an executioner and her flesh
still hatches the maggots. Gently
her thin hands slide the needle
in tepid solitude, marrying

red tulips to daffodils. Seeing her
huddled, you know she's waiting
and has let the hunting horns of youth
pass on with the wind. Her fingers
have stiffened, tired of rousing
earth in the back yard for live flowers.

In age the cat is tiresome with rashes.
She will be half-glad when air
catches dead fur and her spade shakes up
harsh soil for the grave. She waits for bells
to throw the year onto the
centuries' heap like a sack of rotten wood.

I never counted the generations between us.
Like seagulls, the years wing
out of mind and clear the vista from the beach
for fancy. I amble to the hem
of foam, do not guard against
trampling too common fossil shells.

Dinghies hesitate with the swell
like the rowboats you fixed
into telescope sharpness as they prowed
for sand and palms. The vessel perched
safely, too far out for war-canoes. The chaplain
lipped hasty prayers and you

checked manacles for black wrists.
Or did you pay sheikhs for pre-packaged
underdogs, circulate your pipe,
and suck by native right at harem lips?
Your employer's profit and loss is all
the yellowed ink I can strain at.

The figures unlocked once
to rage in a clipped letter. The ship
had caught on a sandbank. You led
two boats of crew to the sunset. The cargo
did not know that they had foundered, shook
chains for tiny biscuit. When waves eased

planks apart the mouths you had trained
in fasting were frozen against the light.
The letter summed costs and cashiered you
with a tantrum. You and your chaplain stayed
on the first British island you beached at,
bought slaves, tamed rain-forest, moralised your lives.

You died chief magistrate. They wrote you
into a wreathed tombstone, sculpted you
beneath orange-trees as one pillar of a humane
empire and faith. Your effigy still makes
the casual visitor question. Myself, I air you,
ancestor, at parties, half-ashamed.

A stitch in time, they'd say, when they mended
microscopic rents in dress uniforms
and struggled to fix the date former
sea-going selves made out some atoll.

They'd force on me, pressganged with yarns, the worth,
from shallops up, of learning sailmaking,
though they knew prick of needles could not
shape all one's life. I would tack the talk

back to the antipodes or Arctic.
In the end they must have given my soul
up for lost: practical tips got thrown
overboard for good. I was the steam

and deck-chair generation; my stomach
must be mechanically stabilised.
But when their eyes doddered I took on
their darning to hear more vagaries.

Earth stitched over them in turn. Sea-breeze rubs
at their ranks, tombstoned above the harbour,
while I always think better safe than
sorry, hold mys sons back from the brink.

The Seaside

Powerboats skim water into foam
with braggart speed. A few arms, out of their depth,
may flail but most move flawless, sure they'll keep
our heads bobbing in dependable air.
We do not risk the bends like the skindivers
who flow across televisions past the rainbow fish
we recognise from their mouthing for space
at aquarium glass. It's left to dreams to push us
under. There we jolt back from sharks, are lacerated
by sudden coral, and edge nervously
among ships' ghosts which unearthly shoals have claimed.
Clutching our trophies for grim life,
we tear past huge suckered tentacles
and surface, blinking, between tortured sheets.

Mammoth
The recovery of the first mammoth from Siberia, 1901

i
Young, I had left dreams of such creatures,
been coddled into dried eyes and calmness.
Later I perused skulls regularly,
the debris of hardly-recognised ancestors' feasts:
the teeth, though lovingly cleaned and a herbivore's,
did not need the reinforcement of femurs and tusks
to chew past the sanity of pencilled reconstructions
and neatly-scaled men
to those nightmare tramplings.
       Nothing, however,
could prepare for this enacting, this forced
retreat from the ways of pen and paper.

ii
I laughed when I recognised the ungainly head and neck
ridged above the river-bank. Digging soon taught
respect. When eventually the broken forelegs
were rescued from mud, I felt one could have kissed it
back to life. We hacked the meat
for the dogs as it thawed,
having measured coarse hair and depth of perfect fat.

Any fantasies of carting it wholesale
our arrival had dispersed into cool air.
But it wasn't just tonnage: although undigested grass
still filled the belly, the knives started to bite
decay. We were thankful to pull bone from bone,
label and stack them on sledges,
let the guides lead the horses.
       The blizzard
surprised us into winter. We scared wolves away
with gunshots, turned hunters. When fireside games
had shrunk into embers, the limbs
took on dark life. Now, mucus threatens
to freeze. We ponder compasses
but have to toss copecks for direction.
Freshly-furred, we rub sticks
to flame each evening.

Tyrolean Festival

For the bishop's annual visit
they had brushed the square like a church-floor,
founded an altar on the dais
by the uniform gold letters
on the war-memorial. Standards which swayed
with medals identified
the contingents of each local village, formal
as platoons until they shared schnapps
to out-perfume candle and censer.
At the elevation of the Host
they presented disused firepieces
to ex-sergeants' brusque monosyllables
and two gaffers fired the touch holes of ordnances
trained for heaven.
               I photographed
girls in white blouses
trimmed with fastidious blood-red,
then climbed to the ceremonial chickens
stabbed with spits in mountain forest. Boozed,
we revelled in the innocuous shadows of firs and pines.

Toad
On a theme of Corbière

Tonight is like the vacuum
above a glass's mercury. Moon
plates with aluminium the dull hints
of day's green bushes. Singing tombed there,
muted like a trombone's bell
by the tree. Glugs down to silence. And
there it is, suggesting a squat shadow
in the two-dimensional dark—toad.
Why did you jump? Why are you breathing
like a piston? Just me rubs shoulders with you,
your faithful batman. Look. Short back and sides.
No wings. Nightingale of mire.
'It's singing, stop that bloody—' Why?
Can't you see that boss-eye, a speck
from here, glint? . . . No, slunk off,
cold, to shrink under its habitual
stone. . . . 'Night. . . . That toad—is me.'

Thumb-Nail

Take my right thumb-nail.
So thick that, squeezed or battered,
it is pink marble, does not deign to attend.

But connive with scissors to trim its growth and you could
be rending the quick. Carapace poised
resolute as Etna over naked nerves.

III. CHÉNIER IN PRISON

Chénier, French aristocrat and poet, was imprisoned and guillotined during the French Revolution. This sequence uses passages from the 'Iambes', a group of poems he wrote while in prison.

i.

When the butcher opens his cavern, shepherd and dog
and the rest of the flock do not inform themselves
of the sheep's fate. The girls who garnished it,
alive, with prize ribbons and flowers, feel
not a jot for it as they slice through its tender flesh.

I ought to have known I would find the same lot in this
abyss. Let's get used to being the forgotten.
We hang by bleeding hooks, wait to be served
to the royal People. What can friends do?
Yes, a word and grasped hand would have soothed across these bars;

perhaps money for the executioners. But then,
it's all precipice. They've the right to clutch at air.
Live happy, despite. . . . Don't rush in my tracks.
Bound up in prosperity, I myself
may have turned away. Now luck's turned. Live, friends. Rest in peace.

ii. The Speech

They say the silent ice she maintains
at the normal foolery melted and boiled
when the breakfast papers served with her coffee
the jumble this time-server orated,
this barbarian's effort at verbal rape.

They say too—but I know our wags treat
the generally charming and self-controlled
to vilification. They like to think she
added—half under her breath—unsubtle
broadsides of abuse to reproaches manly

enough to make gasp. Curses would fit
the theme skin-tight, but not the lips, dear, I could
adulate with absurd metaphor. These men
share none of your tongue. Don't learn theirs. It's base
anger which vindicates their flagrant volleys.

iii. The Massacre

I suppose the newsprint's faithful, that twenty boats,
planks fugitive with rot, were in fact
requisitioned, that these hundreds were herded
and launched to split wood, drop, and display
just chained hands hooking a second
at the ripples for this general's laughter.

Mind you, any night the free can see dandy clerks,
judge and jury laugh round club tables,
flushed with more than mere champagne, stammer today's
murders, tomorrow's hopes. Here and there
venal girls dart, suck at hand, mouth,
and, refugees, try their bedmates' assassins.

iv.

They live, however. It's as if we would trap
imaginary sunbeams in sieves. Cry
for a moon we do not see. A poet's helpless:
my wrists too chafe in mockeries
of bracelets. No Lord of Hosts
rumbles, no angels flash down vengeance lightning.

It's cold comfort to hope I can denounce them
when my head's been nicked off to hell's judges.
Make me live then. No matter how deep they have hid,
I'll search the gulfs, leap, grab them, armed
with my art. The chisel can
eschew the out-dated sparkle of heroes,

tackle degradation. At least the future
may flinch. . . . A proverb declares that remorse
expiates. What remorse wrenches their sleep? This noose
I splice and twine for them must catch
infection. Mere man, I curse
that you can atone but once for debris' groans.

v.

Like the last flick of breeze at dusk, my ink tries
again. Maybe before the minutes
have limped their pegged-out sixty-yard course
these words will have been forced to give up the feeble
ghost and my bawled name have shaken these floors,
bound me and hauled me through jeering crowds.

Well, it's been too long, whatever memories
of warm hands return to see me off.
Runaway fear and sham lord it here,
wiggling every contour like queens of striptease.
Yet the dungeoned victim near death's casket
can keep his chin up, glitter with words

for bitter humanity though the stars say
he'll never touch arms. To die happy
I must knead these executioners
in the mud they smear laws in. Justice doubles up,
retches at their incense: she will surely
conserve me till I've shot all my bolts.

This pen's my artificial respiration:
it lets me escape the invisible
ratchets grief turns inside me. I know
there's a pack of good exemplars, and I am far
from the first evangelist these courts shamed.
These girls, though, their hair has not breathed scents. . . .

My life's water would have been dead without words
to breathe upon it. Nothing could then
be preserved of a heart so famished
it wants the rôles reversed, the lash in its own tensed
hands. As it is, one day poring scholars
may pick at pity over these hymns of praise.

vi.

Oh yes, we live. Dishonoured. Well? We had
no option: the dishonoured do nod off on some food.
And even here, as we attend the axe
in death's pen, you have fine flourishes
of goo-goo letters. We can see

husbands and lovers bilked daily. The same
pounce towards steadying dice or the flaunt of raised skirts.
Endless rounds of jokes and ditties. Balloons
bounced against ceiling and pane like those
dreary party members' harangues.

Some bawl, quickly switch to test frothy smiles
over tankards—in drill for politics.
                                        The grill rasps.
They warble names to honour the axe's
godhead. We who remain shudder out
detained breath, resume normal play.

IV. CATCH A FALLING STAR

The stars are setting and the caravan
Starts for the dawn of nothing.
Edward Fitzgerald

i. Robbie's Funeral

The Norman church splays onto buttresses of wood:
stone abraded by air's stroking and buffets
is to be straightened.
                              The glint of black shoes
clasps at dank turf. The vapid obsequies
emphasise the loss. When our circle unstiffens
for tears or murmurs, and fragments
through conserved lichgate
and icy clerical right hand,
we know that roughly-bedded clods
will stifle wreaths and coffin after the decent
minutes. Mists of our breath spiral
and are erased by winter's torpid sun.

Little Nell, he called me, of Troy. When I nursed
a doll's-house, I used to pout, tightening
my chin nearer to the primness
of a brick wall behind which I attended
to my stubborn flowerbeds.

I have always preferred my name to match
my untrimmed blonde locks which I stroked,
winking at cousins who blossomed
with voices cracked like novices' trombones.

Forgiveness came easily when he conjured toast and jam
from a napkin while I sat on the high chair.
Once my glass showed, though, studious hours of sheening hair,
how could I pummel irritation
lightly onto his shoulder-blades? 'Come on, Nell,'
he said, 'it wouldn't flicker one hair-tip
on a rabbit's tail.' Robbie looked strong
as his plane. Relatives smiled me on,
hands pocketed, staid on tarmac.
The cockpit glass glared through warm air, outstared
my eyes. I promenaded my best grin.
His stretched arm crutched me up
into the seat. I safety-belted myself
to fate. Then the cockpit slammed.

iii. Aerobatics

Pulled to the sky several times, I took
it all in my stride, although I never dared
tug in war with the joy-stick. I sat back
while he modulated aphelion
and perihelion round the radar mast.

It seemed safe as planets while clouds swivelled
to our feet. When our noses shot straight down to
walls of powder-leaves or grass, I might catch
breath in my stomach's stormed gravity, gasp
''Bout time to touch down.' 'You'll never touch down'

and he'd pull out of the dive so we all
but skimmed the grease from my father's ducking crown.
King of fuselage, Robbie would regain
his stronghold of clouds. Dead faith would chant how
pudgy cumuli of cherubs grip him now.

iv. The Reporters

Yes, yes, I knew him. You know that
well, like the serifs or shorthand
ripple of lines and dots
in which you chain war or the latest in necklines.

Haven't these peers, his patrons, bloomed
with enough tinted eulogy,
stemming from creaseless shirts,
to stifle questions once and for all with garlands?

Just a word then. Whatever noise
his flying has made among you,
he was at heart as shy
as a chrysalis. Extended himself in wings

and engines as he regarded
his mere self as so much quicksand,
no solidity man's
foot could rest on. He'd have wanted his death like this,

a shooting star of flame and most
of his body burnt into smoke
before the mauled plane pulped
into the ground. Not heroism; he could never

have faced retirement to drafting
wings on paper and fond daddyhood. . . .
Sorry, I can't linger
for questions. My feelings? My dear sir, go to hell.

v. Maps

Homer questioned with trembling feet
contours of loose stone for equilibrium
on his way to chant to a quaffing chieftain
how Hector consumed dust

and Achilles was felled by the
dandy's flagrant arrow. At least he knew
a hierarchy of hell in which to fit
heroes ousted from feats.

Light-years between constellations
have since then blasted such myths. I can't send
Robbie underground to have slackened muscles
draped with oil for wrestling

in plains where spring always dazzles
with bowl-shaped flowers, nor can dog Latin
plainsong call up shyly (it's not like thumbing
a doorbell) his spirit

to courier me round his new home.
Memories alone spice. And while I can
trap novae in maps, our earthbound love can have
no sure cartography.

vi. Seductress

Several times a lover had departed
with apologetic faithlessness
while my father's arm
folded round my shoulders, insinuating
eligible marriage.
                    I rather liked
to be a *femme fatale*, rest from reducing
the universe to symbols, and calculate
my fourth seduction. Once in a while
it was good, uncaging the archaic nanny-goat, lust,
letting her swagger round the playground and go crazy
about the newest amusement. So when Robbie flew back
from two years in the States, winter evenings
of cribbage with granny had warmed the ice away,
stamped its drops into the hearth-rug,
and had the whole thing planned. Intricate fantasy
would be made flesh. I felt old enough now
to lay morsels before his glad eye.

When he rang the doorbell, he had brought for me
trinkets in floral wrappings. His smile
opened out to flatter little Nell. Behind him
our stiff parade of tulips relaxed
their bright cups under a breeze of sun.

vii. Testing, Testing

He was the quasar which activated
the radio telescope of my emptiness.

We incarnated sex-manuals, then designed
new positions as if drafting
efficiency of fuselage and wings.
When he launched from bed to nosedive
in a new plane, our next experiment
would suspend animation, pinned
to its drawing-board, faithful until his return
brought the kiss of life.

That the T.V. networks sent his goggled image
through Europe's air was to us
like the moon to another, unseeing galaxy.

viii. The Tightrope

New summer clothes lay against our skin.
We stooped as I tended the houseplants (having added
the regulation drops of mineral food
to the small watering-can), then let the sofa
cosset us. We inhaled aerosol flykiller
and discussed a modern jeremiad, swirling
the prospect of man's doom like vintage wine
round our mouths. In a professional way
I'd met cataclysms often, working to deduce
how our planet would pant or yell its last,
how our galaxy's perpetual tarantella
would stop, and whether another universe
stood by in the wings to storm in
when ours expired. I'd always known
eons would have flaked my corpse away
long before the event.
                              I water
the houseplants daily, living in the stench
of his extinct limbs. I think we walk blind
in wrong knowledge the tightrope, uncertainty.

ix. Casualties

Two world wars, decades of military research
were capsuled in that last prototype,
but, as the crowd's uplifted faces watched him
take off, Europe's technology faded out of mind:
warheadless for public show, he was my soul
spiralling far above the past and future
casualties of the century
in love's languid high summer.

Even Samson for all his slaughter of Philistines
can do nothing against the fall of autumn leaves,
must lie boxed under snow.

x. Symphony

My metronome legs give time
to an imagined orchestra:
allegro. I sense male London behind.

Between movements the sunday Serpentine
coolly watches me adjust my hair.
Slowly I resume, stirred
by their unseen footfalls.

I am Pied Piperess. Like kids
they come with me into the subway from the Park,
and there I leave them: my *scherzo* must twist and rock
unaccompanied to Rob's door and the final. . . .

The electric fire stares drily.
I dare not stand to look
through snow-wet windows. Shoulders and head
bend over my breasts.

xi. The Pool

I have wept no Atlantic breakers.
Tears cannot be gathered in test-tubes
held gingerly between finger-tips
and recorded in millilitres. My dry grief
stays a chest of rock round stagnant water.

Words will not blast it free
or methodically bore through so that it gushes
as from a well. Words will not mirror
what rock hides. Love has no epistemology,
cannot be poured into charts like my adored planets.

xii. A London Square

All round there's a corset
of three-storey
houses, coeval.
Only the gradations
of the dirt slumbering
on white paint
keep these fronts distinct.

In the square's trim paddock
behind hedge, trees
and the minute mesh
of green fencing, children
play babes-in-the-wood: big
sister (eight)
soothes cries like mummy.

Between, this road, its turns
an R.S.M.'s
ideal. I can't step
into flat or grass, but
I am free. Free to leave
and keep to
what lone roads I will.

xiii. Promenade

Clean as equations,
these sunday pairs whose siamese-twin shadows
slant towards senior citizens
propped on the promenade seats.

A hundred yards away ripple foams into ripple
into land. Despite the cold, my children too might
have recalled spading sand-walls against tide
and laughing when dad grew foolish,

shovelling half-ounces. Up here,
where sea-wall thwarts lunge of high water,
young arm dissolves round shoulder or waist.
I know how x and y can scent

only each other's skin, ignore the future
solution into figures of middle-age.
I have myself avoided such a warning
that love's panacea can be deadened

as I am now, poker-faced to suppress
this bloody hand I'm left with, gloved fingers
pins and needles without his curls. I understand
how even when January is fanged

with frost, echoing some childhood horror, love
must be aired like washed clothes or a tentative
quadratic, must be shown proof against
sharp salt air and such questioning as mine.

xiv. If Only

I suppose years of 'If only'
would have come to smother. As it was,
when the follicles of his wrist tingled
like stamens under my gentle nails,
I was at sixes and sevens. His enlivened breath
always had the memory of others'
perfumes. His eyes' glint
did not mirror my hope of surer permanence
than the planes he tested and handed over
to any mortal's pilotage.
He could never see how I twined
his hair round my knuckle, slid it up
like a wedding-ring, and imagined my penny
curl to the base of a wishing-well.

xv. Huntress

Desk, ink melt into interplanetary voids
within atoms, where odd unseen electrons
amble round unseen nuclei
which fragment further, like wheat plucked and rolled
between a boy's fingers till grains
eddy on glaring wisps
of breeze from human focus.

The Chinese boxes of uncertainty
have always teased me in equations and graphs
that just fail to lassoo
the chamois which shy from chains
of my brain. Yet my zoo
finally shows new beasts
cringing from crowds' insight.

But this yeti stays shapeless. Its tracks
melt, flee my faithless prayers.
Would-be Amazon of science, I keep seeking
consolation's isotopes. Robbie's few
recovered limbs cuddle mother earth.

xvi. The Car

The car leaks. The out-of-date body
fifteen years ago terrified the thatch
of hamlets with (a lot for those days)
my father's sixty-five m.p.h.

Brilliant metal has been dented,
beaten back to shape, and received a graft
of new flesh where shock was too much.
The lyricism of suspension has gone.

As for myself, there'll be spring seasons,
doubtless, in the lass yet. The car ignores
the oil rainbows it's left behind
on tarmac, bumps on, zombie metal.